D1560273

COLD RIVER

Other books by Joan Larkin

Housework

A Long Sound

JOAN LARKIN

Joan Larkin (signature)

COLD
RIVER

POEMS

*For Marian
with love
& admiration,
Joan
11-22-97*

PAINTED LEAF PRESS

NEW YORK CITY

Acknowledgements

Grateful acknowledgement is made to the following periodicals
in which some of these poems first appeared, at times in differ-
ent forms: *American Poetry Review, Global City Review, Hanging
Loose, OutWeek, The American Voice, The Brooklyn Review;* and
to the editors of the following anthologies: *The Arc of Love,
Last Call: Poems on Alcoholism, Addiction, and Deliverance,
The Key to Everything, The New Fuck You, The Poetry of Sex,
The Wild Good: Lesbian Photographs and Writings on Love,
The Zenith of Desire, Things Shaped in Passing: More "Poets for
Life" Respond to the AIDS Pandemic.*

Special thanks: Doug Atwood, Beatrix Gates, Michael Klein,
Kate Larkin, John Masterson, Honor Moore, Carl Morse,
Eileen Myles, Nina Newington, Gerry Gomez Pearlberg,
Margaret Robison, Paul Selig, Bill Sullivan, David Trinidad,
Steve Turtell, Jean Valentine.

Library of Congress Cataloging-In Publication Data

Larkin, Joan
      Cold river : poems / Joan Larkin.
      p.   cm.
      ISBN 0-96515585-4 (alk. paper)
      I. Title.
PS3562.A724C6   1997
811' .54 --dc21

Cover Painting: *Portal, 1991* by Denis O'Sullivan
Book Design by John Masterson
Printed in USA

In memory:

Celia Moffitt

Denis O'Sullivan

CONTENTS

One

WASTE NOT

We're using every bit of your death.
We're making a vise of your mouth's clenching and loosening,
an engine of your labored breathing,
a furnace of your wide-open eyes.

We've reduced you to stock, fed you to the crowd,
banked the pearl of your last anger,
stored the honey of your last smile.

Nothing's left in your mirror,
nothing's floating on your high ceiling.
We're combing pockets, turning sleeves,
shaking out bone and ash,
stripping you down to desire.

Your beloved has folded your house into his—
I'm wading the swift river, balancing on stones.

INVENTORY

One who lifted his arms with joy, first time across the finish line
    at the New York marathon, six months later a skeleton
    falling from threshold to threshold, shit streaming from
    his diaper,
one who walked with a stick, wore a well-cut suit to the opera,
    to poetry readings, to mass, who wrote the best long poem
    of his life at Roosevelt Hospital and read it on television,
one who went to 35 funerals in 12 months,
one who said *I'm sick of all you AIDS widows,*
one who lost both her sisters,
one who said *I'm not sure that what he and I do is safe, but we're
    young, I don't think we'll get sick,*
one who dying said *They came for me in their boat, they want me
    on it, and I told them Not tonight, I'm staying here with James,*
one who went to Mexico for Laetrile,
one who went to California for Compound Q,
one who went to Germany for extract of Venus' flytrap,
one who went to France for humane treatment,
one who chanted, holding hands in a circle,
one who ate vegetables, who looked in a mirror and said
    I forgive you,
one who refused to see his mother,
one who refused to speak to his brother,
one who refused to let a priest enter his room,
one who did the best paintings of his life and went home from
    his opening in a taxi with twenty kinds of flowers,
one who moved to San Francisco and lived two more years,
one who married his lover and died next day,
one who said *I'm entirely filled with anger,*
one who said *I don't have AIDS, I have something else,*
one with night sweats, nausea, fever, who worked as a nurse,
one who kept on studying to be a priest,
one who kept on photographing famous women,
one who kept on writing vicious reviews,

one who kept going to AA meetings till he couldn't walk,
one whose son came just once to the hospital,
one whose mother said *This is God's judgment,*
one whose father held him when he was frightened,
one whose minister said *Beth and her lover of twelve years were devoted as Ruth and Naomi,*
one whose clothes were thrown in the street, beautiful shirts and ties a neighbor picked from the garbage and handed out at a party,
one who said *This room is a fucking prison,*
one who said *They're so nice to me here,*
one who cut my hair and said *My legs bother me,*
one who couldn't stand, who said *I like those earrings,*
one with a tube in his chest, who asked *What are you eating?*
one who said *How's your writing? Are you moving to the mountains?* who said *I hope you get rich.*
One who said *Death is transition,*
one who was doing new work, entirely filled with anger,
one who wanted to live till his birthday, and did.

ALTHEA

The baby lasted one whole year.
He lay there in the coma, lips like a little knot.
I went after work and bathed him.
I always talked to him.
Then my twin got the virus
and looked it, a skeleton
in a red scarf. Althea,
she'd say, I'm going to die.
And I'd say No.
By then I was sober,
but my brain was on fire:
I'd put my head in the toilet
and flush—ten, fifteen times—
the water was so cold.
My mother'd say when I came
home from my son, Althea,
how do you do it?
I didn't know she was asking
for herself How do you lose
your child? And I didn't answer,
I didn't know then
how the dead live.
Only how to sponge
my son's delicate ribs
my twin's skinny thighs
sweating in the white sheet.
Only how to grab one day
by the wrists and hold on,
whatever is on its breath.

PHOTO

A winter afternoon lengthens on your pillow.
Head propped, hair fanned out around your forehead,
dark lesions on the bridge of your nose,
you're lying back, loose hospital gown
a blizzard of blue snow. Eyes bluer.
Your mouth open in a smile or grimace,
not yet vomiting blood like rich black
oil from the well of your animal self.
Not yet the open mouth I saw in a photo like this one—
Peter Hujar newly dead, face of a Mexican Christ. You
are alive, and it's still your mouth, Francis,
framed by your new beard—
soft, sexual—I could put my fingers through it.
A shock of chest-hair lies
across the loose skin of your throat,
creased flesh he kissed who laid his cheek there,
tongue along your breastbone tasting your salt.
But death is in progress—
your slow, arduous climb; its rude surprises:
blood, shit, vomit, in rooms full of friends;
falling, forgetting;
your lost rhythms of sex and running;
your long body a mask for bone.
I'm looking at your photo, Francis—
it took three years.
You, looking at your death.
Your powerful, candid eyes.

IN TIME OF PLAGUE

When you sit with me I forget
how thin you looked, waiting,
like a boy in shorts; how the dark
look crossed your face,
an eclipse casting its flank of shadow.
We're sitting in light, smiling,
me saying, *Odd not to live here now.*
You, *If I get sick*—
You leave your fish uneaten,
rake kale with your fork.
Your polite *If*—I seize it,
break my roll in pieces
as you paint a future hell
where you're helpless against our pity.
I stop eating, hard seed
lodged in my tender gum,
everything in me looking
at you as your face tilts up.
I can't believe you've left the city!
Blood heats my face,
my spine feels cold.
I'd come back—I pray
to mean it. You don't
contradict me; you smile, swallow
water. I notice the young
waiter's full, dark hair,
the sweet, slightly rotten
smell of freesia, as
we look away from each other.

SONNET POSITIVE

Nothing is life-or-death in this slow drive
to Vermont on back roads—lunch, a quick look
at antiques—though he does bring up his grave
and wanting a stone. The road curves; we joke
about the quickest way to ship ashes
to England, and whether he ought to have
himself stuffed, instead, like a bird. He flashes
me a glance that says it's ok, we can laugh
at this death that won't arrive for a while. We pull
over. He's not actually sick yet, he reminds me,
reaching for the next pill. His bag's full
of plastic medicine bottles, his body
of side effects, as he stoops to look at a low
table whose thin, perfect legs perch on snow.

A REVIEW

It wasn't the worst movie
I've seen about AIDS.
Lots of nice family.
Catholics who never flinch
from kissing their infected son.
Nobody saying Do you mind
not holding the baby,
not even the pregnant sister
says I love you, but I can't let you
inject yourself in our house.
Not once does the father cry
Where did we go wrong?
Red ribbon looped in every lapel,
no one afraid their faggot
son will burn for eternity.
No one too queer,
no one crazed from death
after death. No kissing,
nothing scarier than a glimpse
of KS sores like a map
of new islands under
the hero's immaculate shirt.
He's a boyscout who once had sex
in a porn theatre, went there
three times in his life—
no 900 numbers,
subway toilets, sadism,
anger, failure, complexity—
it's a movie, isn't it?
How could I expect him
not to die the minute he says
I'm ready—no weeks
of morphine & oxygen, whispers
at the bedside all night,

exhausted laughter, pleading:
You've got to leave your body;
there's nothing left for it but pain.
It was a six-dollar entertainment,
popcorn spilled in the aisles.
But somewhere in the middle, a scene
in a library. The unshaven
gaunt face, the cheap
watch cap, were yours, Denis.
I saw you staring, stripped
to your fear and wanting to live.
And later, listening to Callas,
the dying man's lifted face
flickering green, red—
pleasure, dementia. Love,
it was your face, & I wept.

THE FAKE

The man in front of me is you
from the back—the same
wrinkled plaid, the same
fine hair, wire rims.
When he turns, I see
his red face—a coarse
copy of your lost health.
The room is hot.
I scan the crowd
for anyone who knew you.

T w o

IN THE DUCHESS
Sheridan Square, 1973

Women swayed together
on that scuffed floor. I stared
at the strong beauty who stood

and shook the tambourine.
The poised waitress poured,
hips pressed against hips—

I drank their half-closed
eyes, half-opened lips,
link bracelets, ease

of illegal dancing. Soon
I'd cut my hair, soon
sharpen cuffs and creases,

burn bold as the stone
butch staring back
in whose smile my fear

and wanting found a mirror.
There, amid booze, smoke,
loud unmerciful music,

my whole body was praying
that now my real life—
molting animal,

new, wet skin—
would come touch me,
and at last, I'd dance.

BEATINGS

They beat me different ways.
My mother was standing
in her light summer suit and hat.
She was late; it was my fault.
She was almost sobbing. A cord
was twisted around her breath,
an animal trying to escape
from her throat. Her knuckles landed
hard on my shoulders, in my ribs and guts.
Her face was close. She was yelling,
yanking me by the hair, and I saw my brother
standing near us in the hall, watching.
Standing and forgetting why he was there
watching and what he liked about it.

I was younger. I think we were all there,
four or five in the kitchen, father home
for supper between shifts. He lifted me
over his knees to hit me. Belt,
brush, or his large hand came down
open and steady on both buttocks, burning
and stinging through thin underpants,
big voice in control, saying This
is for your own good, This
hurts us, This is because we love you.
I cannot remember my crime, only my face
against his knees. His hands, his strong
voice telling me I was loved.

When the man beat me later
in the bed in Brooklyn, the kind man
with big lips and hands, the man
who loved me and beat me
with the same voice, when years later

in the same bed, the thin woman with tattooed
wrists told me I couldn't receive
love, thrusting the dildo till I was
sore and crying *Stop,* she laughing,
shouting I couldn't love her—
it wasn't true. I loved the rising
of their voices—his dark, steady one,
sure, in control, and her demented one
rising like my dead mother's wild voice.

HUNGER

Turned on. Turned off.
I was both, as she smeared the lube
the way you'd spread margarine—
flat hand, quick upturning wrist—
she was a worker.
I was a cut loaf. I was a client
from her child whore time.
I lay thinking how her first sex
was "to get it over with quick
so I could work"—as her mother worked,
as they worked together and alone
learning the quarter where a man
could feed you or kill you.
Her hand on me was firm, a boxer's,
her body narrow, dark, hard.
How ludicrous a cock and harness had seemed before this.
I wanted it and didn't
as she snaked up the bed—
leather, flesh, sweat shining,
eyes like an animal's
staring into me as if she had a right—
that cat I'd watched her seize with both hands
and shake, gazing at its face
and shouting *I love you!*
We lay slant,
mouth on mouth, breast on breast,
clapped together, ringing.
She pressed into me so hard
I could feel my ribs and the bones of my face,
I could feel her impossible hunger.
In the end,
I too arched and reared.

MY BODY

Throat puckered like crepe,
right hand throbbing with arthritis,
right hip permanently higher than left, right leg shorter
      after years of books slung from one shoulder.
One breast smaller, both sagging like Grandma's,
      shriveled around the nipples,
upper arms lumpy, veins in legs varicose,
back freckled from sunburn when I passed out on the beach
      in 1964,
face creasing, still breaking out, hairs bristling from bumps
      I didn't start out with,
nose pitted, burst capillaries on nostrils,
two extra holes pierced in the left ear so I'll never forget
      those months with Sido—thank God I refused the tattoo,
two vaccination scars,
shoulder stiff from fracture in 1986 when I fell on a stone
      floor at Cummington,
skin dotted with—what? moles? age spots? melanoma that
      killed my father?
sagging belly, testament to fear, dieting, birth, abortion,
      miscarriage,
years of fighting booze and overeating still written in my flesh,
small cysts around labia, sparse pubes—not yet like my head
full of grey that first appeared the year I had two jobs
      and pneumonia.
Eyes needing bifocals now, no good for driving at night,
still blue and intense, tired but my best feature—
or maybe it's my hands, strong, blunt, with prominent veins.
Lungs still wheezing after years of asthma and smoking,
all of me still full of groans, sighs, tears,
still responsive to the slightest touch,
grief and desire still with me
though I hardly ever have reason to close the curtains,
naked fool for passion—

and wonder if I'll live alone the rest of my time in this body—
my old friend now,
healed and healed again,
still walking and breathing,
scars faded as thin silver signatures.

WANT

She wants a house full of cups and the ghosts
of last century's lesbians; I want a spotless
apartment, a fast computer. She wants a woodstove,
three cords of ash, an axe; I want
a clean gas flame. She wants a row of jars:
oats, coriander, thick green oil;
I want nothing to store. She wants pomanders,
linens, baby quilts, scrapbooks. She wants Wellesley
reunions. I want gleaming floorboards, the river's
reflection. She wants shrimp and sweat and salt;
she wants chocolate. I want a raku bowl,
steam rising from rice. She wants goats,
chickens, children. Feeding and weeping. I want
wind from the river freshening cleared rooms.
She wants birthdays, theaters, flags, peonies.
I want words like lasers. She wants a mother's
tenderness. Touch ancient as the river.
I want a woman's wit swift as a fox.
She's in her city, meeting
her deadline; I'm in my mill village out late
with the dog, listening to the pinging wind bells, thinking
of the twelve years of wanting, apart and together.
We've kissed all weekend; we want
to drive the hundred miles and try it again.

Three

TO SPIRIT

...God of breathing,
I pray that my mother will make her breakfast and really eat it,
that she will wash herself and walk to the kitchen without falling,
that my brother will shut up about the nursing home,
that she will dress herself in mint and pink polyester,
pay her rent,
take heart medicine,
sleep through the night,
read a book again.

That her friend Sandy will bring soup,
that Mary Hoyt will sit with her,
Marian shop for her,
Meals on Wheels feed her.
That nightmare will not harrow her,
no man frighten her,
my brother not bully her, bully her.

God, do not abandon us in our age
or worse, let condescending children control us.
For choice is the life spirit in her
even as she becomes a child.

And as work is taken from us,
and as home is taken from us,
and as sex is taken from us,
and as the body is taken from us,
and writing is taken
and the mind lightens
and we are divested even of sense—
let Self remain—
and choose—
Spirit, all praise to You—
choose, even on the last day.

JOURNEY

Her bedroom's sour-smelling, hot; the pad
backed with electric-blue plastic, drowned.

She's hunched and grimacing. I'm going home
on the next flight; I smile back, don't

dare be afraid. I ask, How was your night?
I got up once, to go—that's all. Her exhausted

bright eyes are a child's. *Next time,*
I want you to bring me Kate. Her cane's on the floor;

she reaches for it, grabs the nightstand, lifts.
Steadies herself on walls, doorknob, tv.

Staggers. Achieves her end:
the pink bathroom.

HERE

I breathe with her:
the long nothing, then the gasp.
I want to rest between those groans,
those blank stares.
Rest my cheek against her freckled arm,
my face in the cool L of her elbow
watching her neck tense and relax:
half minutes, her mouth sunk open.
I want this to stop.
Look the length of her body,
length of her pale life,
all hollows and soft mounds;
below the pulled-up gown, sparse net of hairs.
Her eyes are closed, she's quiet.
The not breathing lasts less than a minute.
She groans. Then, *Joan!*
Where have you been all afternoon?
Here, I say.

BLUE SLIPPER

Nothing in this day—
not the doe this morning
looking uphill through my windshield
so still I thought she was light;
not the young priest, saying
The place to pray from is God's heart—
I went there a moment when he said it;
not even the road inked with pines,
bright shawl of fog,
hills the color of deep water—
nothing in this world, Mother,
is poised in my mind like the blue slipper
that won't fit your swollen foot.
Good terrycloth scuffs from J. Byron's
I don't think you saw. They came in a clear
plastic envelope. I opened it for you,
wrote your name on the soles with a black
marker. The nurse said *You might as well
throw them away.* Over a year now
I can't get it on you, Mother,
can't get it off.

COLD RIVER

My mother disappeared in a shoddy
pine coffin in the rain
while my brother complained of its cheapness
and one aunt whispered
as I took my turn shoveling
in black clothes and shame.
Before that, she disappeared
in a useless body we fed,
lifted, tortured, four months.
Suddenly the house was full
of thin, rose-painted china.
The valuable ring she'd kept
where they couldn't steal it
felt loose on my middle finger.
The day I phoned from Shelburne,
the nurse whispered to me,
Now her legs are weeping.
I was resting from her long dying.
Mother, I said. I'm in the cabin.
I can hear you—twice
she dragged words to the surface.
I can't forget that voice.
It was my first. The bitter
edge I hated as I grew wild
was the only weapon of the woman
who called me *Daughter.*
Now it's a current in me
like the cold river
I take grief swimming in.

JEWISH CEMETERY, WEST ROXBURY

Inside the city, a city of stone slabs,
acorns dropping on mossed walks.
I find hers at the far end in a walled corner,
a grave bought in the '40s, before the crowds.
I am happy and kneel,
not thinking about the rain
last summer when they opened
the deep trough for her.
Not thinking about her feet
nor my own frozen months.
My working lungs are a wonder to me.
Whatever is left
of flesh, shroud, box
can't hear me,
so I speak openly to the day,
mouth tender with praise
as hers once she forgave me.
I find three muddy stones
to leave in honor of life's hardness.
A beetle forages among them
as I walk to the car
beneath the gift of a daytime moon.

LEGACY

When my mother finally left her body
it was mine to keep
along with her ring,
some blackened silver,
a box of Jewish books.
At first I thought it would be a difficult fit
but here a tuck and there a seam let out
and you'd swear it was made for me.
My freckled throat,
creased stomach,
soft, white hips—
even my thoughts at 3:00 a.m. are hers.
I'm lying here in her body!
She doesn't miss it,
she likes the way I look in it,
winks when I feed it her favorites.
Sunday I'll walk down the aisle at my daughter's wedding
and the thin breasts in grey silk
will be my mother's. Veins in sticky hose,
bunioned feet in shoes that match the dress—
more and more will be hers.
I'll walk past the narrow eyes of those who doubt me
safe in my mother's armor—
faux-pearl choker and stiff, glittering clasp—
as their whispers weave around me
my face wearing her little smile,
her scared eyes shining in triumph.

ROBERT

Right now in Fayetteville
where it's two, not three o'clock,
you're doing what you did then:
driving a rattletrap, maybe
on a road lush with spring green,
or sharpening a Venus drawing pencil
by a river that's slowly drying out.
I see the thin green pencil,
not the hand holding it—
I can't remember your hands.
There's a dog with you, not
the one we had together—
she must be dead ten years.
I see you in worn flannel
and round gold glasses. Those
must be gone, too,
with the hat I hated,
the square brown one with earflaps.
I want to call you on the phone.
Want us in Tucson together, 1962,
before my father died. Before
any of it. I want to be kind this time,
and not just to you.
I want my mother back,
the way she was then:
not thin or grey yet,
not sweet the way she was later,
starting to die. Robert, she forgave me:
for divorcing you, even for writing
that I was queer. She didn't say
she forgave me, she just said,
Oh well, you turned out all right.
I want to call you
in Fayetteville, right now,

so you can say it too: *I love you,*
in your surprising baritone.
I want to say, *Mother,*
please sit with me in the orange kitchen.
I have something to tell you.

Joan Larkin's previous collections of poetry are *Housework* and *A Long Sound.* She co-edited the anthologies *Amazon Poetry* and *Lesbian Poetry* with Elly Bulkin and *Gay and Lesbian Poetry in Our Time* (winner of a Lambda Literary Award) with Carl Morse. She is the author of a prize-winning play, *The Living,* and co-translator with Jaime Manrique of *Sor Juana's Love Poems.* A teacher of writing for many years, she has served on the faculties of Brooklyn, Sarah Lawrence, and Goddard colleges. She is the recipient of a National Endowment for the Arts Creative Writing Fellowship, and currently lives and writes in New York City.

In October 1997 this book was printed by
BookCrafters, Michigan, for Painted Leaf Press.
The text is set in 11 point Garamond.
Design by John Masterson